MW00945682

Martin R. Phillips

ANCIENT

GREECE

Hill Tech Ventures Inc.
Publishing Division | Nanaimo, Canada
Printed in the United States

ANCIENT

GREECE

Discover the Secrets of

Ancient Greece

MARTIN R. PHILLIPS

ABOUT THE AUTHOR

MARTIN R. PHILLIPS

 Martin R. Phillips is an extremely passionate historian, archaeologist, and most recently a writer. Ever since Martin was a young boy he has been fascinated with ancient cultures and civilizations.

In 1990, Martin graduated with distinction from the University of Cambridge with a double major in History and Archaeology. Upon graduation, Martin worked as an archeologist and travelled the world working in various excavation sites. Over the years, while working as an archaeologist, Martin became very well cultured and gained great insights into some of the most historic civilizations to ever exist. This first hand insight into the ancient cultures of the world is what sparked Martin's newest passion, history writing and story telling.

In 2012, Martin decided to retire from archeology to focus on writing. Over the years he has seen and experienced a great deal of fascinating things from all over world. Martin now spends the majority of his free time putting all of his research, experience, and thoughts onto paper in an attempt to share his knowledge of the ancient cultures with the world.

Over the past few years Martin has excelled in his writings. His narrative style has a way of combining the cold hard facts with a story teller's intrigue which makes for an excellent reading experience.

"Live your life to the fullest and enjoy the journey!"

- Martin R. Phillips

TABLE OF CONTENTS

Encompassing over two

individual city...

fascinating fascinate ('fas^{3}n.āt) vb 被迷住
Transfix and hold spellbound

INTRODUCTION

permeate(d) 瀰漫 充滿 'pəmē,āt
seep through
mythology 神話之總稱 mythologies n

Ancient Greece is, without a doubt, one of the most
fascinating cultures that our world has ever seen!
Whether you look at their mythology, their history, or
their philosophy, the Ancient Greek civilization has
permeated our approach to, and understanding of,
the world at large. It is impossible to tell the story of
modern civilization without providing some recogni-
tion to the influence of Greece. act of recognizing or
state of being recognized

The Greek Empire was vast, encompassing over 700
individual city-states, 150-173 of which would form
the Delian League in an effort to combat the onslaught of Persia. How did so many city-states come
together under one rule? With only a fraction joining
the Delian League, how did these city-states *stay* together in times of disagreement and conflict?

There are hundreds, if not thousands of questions
regarding this vast and fascinating civilization. One
could spend years and write many volumes on each
period of the Ancient Grecian culture, history, and
mythology. It has been my pleasure to assemble this
research, and the voice of Greece itself (through reference to its own historians, including Herodotus,

Thucydides, and Xenophon.) I am excited to share with you an admittedly brief look at the civilization we know as Ancient Greece (a full history would take more pages than the unabridged Oxford English Dictionary and the Encyclopedia Britannica combined.)

In this book you will find the history and opinions of the Ancient Greeks. You will discover their truth and their mythology. You will learn of war and peacetime. There are heroes and villains, saints and scoundrels. You will find philosophies that changed the world, and continue to do so even to this day.

For the most part, the contents of this book are arranged topically as opposed to strictly chronologically to allow specific areas of interest in the Ancient Greeks and their civilization to be more easily accessible. However, care has been taken to include the approximate dates of people and events to give you a good idea of the chronology of the content.

The importance of the Greek civilization cannot be overstated. In nearly every facet of our lives, we can find something which had its roots, or took a new turn in Ancient Greece. When you go to the polls to elect an official, you are operating on a Greek principle. When you discuss the nature of life with others, you are performing a modified version of the Greek symposium. Even when you sit down to watch television, or read a book, you often find references to Trojan wars, Sparta and their role in the conflict with the

Persians, the philosophy, or the character of the Greeks.

As you rediscover Ancient Greece, I encourage you to make note of how much of that vast and diverse civilization still lives on throughout our world today.

Thanks again, I hope you enjoy it!

CHAPTER 1

The Beginning

While the earliest portions of what would come to be ancient Greece are largely lost to antiquity, there is still quite a bit that we can deduce from the evidence that we do have.

The era commonly known as ancient Greece began in the 8th century BC and lasted until around the 7th century AD with the end of antiquity. Ancient Greece consisted of a few distinct periods of Greek government and culture. These include the Archaic, Classical, Hellenistic, and Roman periods.

This chapter, however, will give you a brief outline of the time period preceding that of what we commonly call Ancient Greece. Points of focus include: The Neolithic Era, The Bronze Age including the Minoan, Cycladic, and Mycenaean civilizations, and the Greek Dark Age.

The Neolithic Era: 6,800-3,200 BC

While there was activity in the area which would come to be known as Ancient Greece before these periods, The Neolithic era saw the stabilization of the climate, the introduction of farming, stock-rearing, and pottery; and the building of settlements among other important matters.

The last Glacial Period (inaccurately termed the last Ice Age) ended around 8,000 BC, and this led to the advent of more permanent settlements in Greece. Prior to this period, many peoples were nomadic, but with the stabilization of the climate, they were able to build these permanent settlements.

The economy was largely based on a barter system where goods and services were traded for produce from farmers, cattle and other stock, and pottery. This diversification allowed people to focus more on one particular kind of work as they could barter their trade for whatever provisions they needed.

Settlement and the meeting of an individual's daily needs (food, water, etc.) led to the advent of craftsmen. These people were specialists in their particular areas, and trade became a more important facet of everyday life. People turned to outside sources to supplement things which were either unavailable, or in short supply in their given areas, and everyone was able to meet their essential needs without the necessity of traveling from place to place. Neolithic settlements were often fortified, but allowed trade and travel for its citizens.

Although hunting and gathering provided individuals with much more free time than agriculture has, it was also much less efficient. It would take about 1,000 calories of expenditure to obtain 1,000 calories of food, thus surplus was relatively unheard of. People had to move from place to place as nomads in order to ensure that they could hunt and gather enough food to sustain them.

The Neolithic Age is often known as the last period of the Stone Age. Tools were usually made of stone, as well as weapons, building materials, and other necessities as it was extremely plentiful in all areas of the habitable world.

The advent of agriculture, often known as either the agricultural revolution or The Neolithic Revolution, allowed people to remain in one place and actually obtain a surplus of food. Having a food surplus allowed settlements to grow and, although without agriculture people had more time, less use for slave labor, very little impact on their (and subsequently) our environment, Ancient Greece, let alone modern civilization would be impossible in the way we know it.

Aegean Civilization (The Greek Bronze Age): 3,200-1,050 BC

The Aegean civilization is a reference to The Bronze Age settlements of Greece in and around the Aegean Sea. The Aegean Bronze Age started around 3,200 BC, (Aegean Islands around 3,000 BC, and Crete in about 2,800 BC,) although there is a great deal of speculation on the exact dates. Initially, bronze was very expensive, and so it was typically reserved for the wealthy. In fact, the class system of civilization was largely initiated based on the availability of these metals, and who had them.

Due to its initially limited supply, bronze took quite a while to become commonplace, but was generally in use beginning around 2,800 BC. What led to its popularity and widespread use was the fact that bronze was much easier to use than traditional tools, and thus it eventually replaced stone for tools and weapons.

In Greece, The Bronze Age was typified by the expansion of settlements, the development of navigation, the growth of individual dwellings, and further class stratification. During this time, trade became more and more vital to the growth and sustainability of cities and thus found great expansion.

There were three predominant groups in the area of Greece during this time. They were the Minoan, the Cycladic, and the Mycenaean civilizations.

The Cycladic civilization existed from approx. 3,200-2,000 BC. The Cycladic civilization was located on a number of islands in the Aegean Sea, most notably around the Cyclades. Although not much is known about the inner-workings of this civilization, we do have archaeological evidence which suggests that they were seafaring people who were notable for sculpture. Some evidence shows signs of copper-working. Their sculptures have been found in various places in the Greek area, including Knossos on the island of Crete. With the exception of Delos, this group drifted into the background with the advent of Cretan palace-culture.

Like the Cyclades, there isn't much specific knowledge of the Minoan civilization. In fact, the term Minoan was coined by Arthur Evans, and is taken from the mythical King Minos, a son of Zeus and Europa. The Minoans controlled many of the Greek Islands, most notably Crete

The Minoan Civilization on Crete lasted from approx. 2,700 BC to 1,450 BC, and began in the city of Knossos. The island was rich in natural resources, and the Minoans took great part in overseas trading. They were largely merchants and fishermen, although they made use of lumber for trading and building their sea craft. There were craftsmen, and traders, indicating a proliferation of craft specialization. The Minoan civilization of Crete was invaded by the Mycenaeans in about 1,400 BC. Their written language is known as Linear A, and is presently indecipherable.

The Mycenaeans, often referred to as "Proto-Greeks," were a Helladic (of mainland Greece) civilization from approx. 1,600-1,050 BC, although they did come to control many of the Greek Islands during the span of their civilization. They did speak an early form of Greek and had two predominant forms of written language known as Linear A and Linear B. While Linear B was largely deciphered in the 1950s, Linear A remains indecipherable. As there are no written historical accounts that we're presently aware of about the Mycenaeans *by* the Mycenaeans, historians have been able to trace their culture through by tracking their pottery.

The Mycenaeans get their name from archaeologists of the 19th century from the name of their capitol city of Mycenae, which is located about 56 miles (90 kilometers) southwest of Athens. Mycenae is also well-known for being the city from which the mythical Agamemnon ruled in Homer's Iliad. In The Iliad, the Trojan wars were fought between the peoples of Mycenae and the city of Troy. The storyline of the Greek poet Homer The Iliad beginning nine years after the beginning of the mythical Trojan War.

The Mycenaeans were bold traders, fierce warriors, and phenomenal engineers made up of numerous cities connected by a common language and culture. The people were governed by a singular king who had ultimate power to levy taxes, and generally govern the people. These kings were extremely wealthy

Mycenaean buildings were usually built atop a hill and were made of stone, both of which suggest that they were designed with defense in mind. Some of these structures are still standing today, including the Lion's Gate in Mycenae.

The economy was a palace-economy, a moneyless system where goods are stored in a central location and doled out to the people as needed. These goods were largely the products of farming and trade.

The collapse of the Mycenaean civilization occurred sometime between 1,200 and 1,050 BC. The reasons for the collapse are unknown; however the cities of this civilization were either abandoned or, in many cases, destroyed. Speculation about the collapse includes rebellion, invasion, or possibly a widespread natural disaster.

The Greek Dark Ages (or Early Iron Age) 1,200-800 BC

This period in Greece was largely characterized by the loss of cities and a great loss of writing. However the culture may have lost many of its important facets, iron working began to come about, and iron would eventually replace bronze as the predominant metal of tools and weapons, etc.

With the loss of cities, many of the people relied upon herding to fulfill their needs. The surplus of food had largely dissipated with the dissolution of the Mycenaean civilization and their many cities.

At some point between 1,100 and 950 BC, something often referred to as The Dorian Invasion occurred. The Dorian Invasion is a term often used to explain the transition between the pre-classical language, writing and culture to that which was predominant in classical Greece, specifically the area around Sparta.

The classical mythos behind this event is that the descendants of Hercules returned to reclaim the lands which Hercules had held during his lifetime. Much more likely is that it wasn't an actual invasion at all, but a migration which occurred over a very long period of time.

CHAPTER 2

The Pantheon of the Gods

To understand what the religion of Ancient Greece was to its people is to understand a great deal about the people themselves. These gods and goddesses along with the mythos attached to them would dominate Greek knowledge and philosophy for centuries.

The Greek Religion was polytheistic (belief in multiple gods) and these gods were said to interact with people on a constant basis. Many women would claim that they had gotten pregnant through intercourse with one of the chief deities, often Zeus himself. Others claimed that their injuries or diseases were cured by the gods' own intervention. Still more attributed military victories, social and political success, acts of nature, and various other positive and negative personal or collective experiences to the intervention of these gods.

Rather than simply provide a list of the gods and their attributions, it seems fitting to give a closer account of the chief gods and their powers, their hierarchical structure, and effects on Ancient Greek civilization. Along with the gods themselves, the religion, morality, and general mythology bear investigation.

The gods were not the omnipotent, ambivalently benevolent gods which dominate the cultural landscape today. The gods behaved and appeared much more like the people who worshipped them. The gods weren't just jealous of the others, they were also believed to engage in (consensual and nonconsensual) sexual intercourse on a regular basis, and had the same human emotions and imperfections as the people who worshipped them.

There was a power structure to the pantheon with Zeus as its king. Zeus was the youngest son of Cronus and Rhea and had a modicum of control over all of the other gods. However, many myths and legends have the other gods sneaking around behind Zeus's back and causing all sorts of mischief. Zeus controlled the weather, and wielded lightning bolts. He is said to have ruled the Olympians (in this case, the inhabitant gods of Olympus) as a father ruled his family.

Although in most traditions Zeus is married to Hera, his frequent sexual exploits resulted in his various children with other deities and, quite often, with mortal women as well as in the case of Heracles (often called Hercules.) In most instances of his intercourse with goddesses, the children were born as new gods or goddesses such as Athena, Hermes, and Ares (to name a brief few.) His affairs with mortal women, however, often resulted in beings such as Heracles who were a hybrid of hero and god.

The gods of the ancient Greeks often presided over various functions of nature, such as Helios as the god who controlled the movement of the sun; and Poseidon who ruled over the sea. Other times, the gods were behind different emotions or states of being such as Aphrodite who ruled over love; and Uranus who was the god of the sky, or the heavens.

Other notable entities included the primordial gods such as Chaos, the father of life, the universe, etc.; and Aether who was the god of the pure upper air of the Olympians (not to be confused with the normal air that mortals breathe.)

There were the Titans who were a powerful race of gods who spawned (and were subsequently overthrown by) the Olympians such as Mnemosyne who was the personification of memory and was mother to the muses; and Cronus (often Kronos) who was the father of Zeus and led the revolt against Uranus (the sky.)

Cronus is particularly of interest in Greek mythology in that he feared losing power to his children as his father had lost power to him. He therefore ate five of his six children one by one. The sixth child, Zeus, was saved by his mother (Cronus's wife and sister) Rhea when, after Zeus's birth, she presented a stone to Cronus, swaddled in cloth so that he would be unaware that he was not consuming his new son. When Zeus grew up, he forced Cronus to imbibe a potion which caused the latter to vomit up the children which he had devoured. Thus, his siblings were reborn. The siblings: Demeter, Hestia, Hera, Hades, Poseidon and Zeus joined together to wage war against their father and the rest of the Titans, eventually bound and launched into oblivion.

Other gods and godlike beings included The Muses who were said to be the goddesses of inspiration. There were Nymphs who were divine beings who animated different aspects of nature. There were the Giants, and their relatives the Cyclopes who were one-eyed giants. Along with these, there were also various beings consisting of half-humans or human-like beings such as satyrs (half-man and half-goat,) centaurs (half-man and half horse,) and gorgons (hideous female creatures with hair made of live, venomous snakes,) of which Medusa is a well-known example.

Many books could be and have been written about the various gods, titans, etc. What is important is how the belief in these gods affected the Greeks in their culture and in their daily lives.

Greek morality was largely based on striving toward moderation, as most vices were considered acceptable in-and-of themselves, while taking these things to extremes, such as overeating, excessive drinking, etc. would lead one to great error.

Hubris (extreme pride to the point of delusion) was the most feared and despised of vices, as it was seen as a chief cause behind things such as rape, murder, and betrayal. Pride itself wasn't considered a negative thing, however when it reached the point of hubris, it had reached the point of being out of control, and was often personified as pridefulness and an overestimation of one's abilities to the exclusion of others' rights.

Many of the Greek city-states were based upon a belief that a particular deity was the city's patron. Who the people chose as their city-state's patron shows a lot about the focus of that city-state. Athens for instance was named for their patron goddess Athena. The city was therefore primarily concerned with education and knowledge, as Athena was the goddess of wisdom. Sparta had two: Ares, and Artemis. Ares, the god of war signified Sparta's focus on military might while Artemis, the god of the hunt among other things.

Many of the Greek myths were used to explain natural phenomena. One such myth is that of Persephone and Hades. It was said that Persephone, the unspeakably gorgeous daughter of Demeter, goddess of fertility, was working in a field one day when the earth cracked open, and she was taken to the underworld by Hades. For nine days, Demeter searched for her daughter, neglecting the crops of the earth which caused them to die off. Zeus, seeing that humanity could not survive without Demeter to make the earth fertile again, intervened, and demanded that Hades release Persephone to be with her mother. Hades agreed to release Persephone so long as she hadn't eaten anything while in the underworld. However, Hades had tricked Persephone into eating pomegranate seeds. It was finally decided that while Persephone would be allowed to live with her mother during most of the year, she would have to return to Hades for three months. During the time in which Persephone was with her mother, crops flourished; however during her three months with Hades, the world became cold and barren. Such was the explanation for winter.

The Olympic Games were originally established to pay tribute to Zeus. Along with these games, which were held in the city of Olympia, animals were sacrificed to Zeus. Priests would then take the blood of the slaughtered animals and spread it on an altar in the temple of Zeus to further honor their deity.

One more tradition in Greek religion was the development of mystery schools. These schools or cults were each dedicated to a particular deity. For instance, the Eleusinian mystery school was a cult of Demeter. Anyone who had clean hands, in other words had not committed a blood offense such as murder, was allowed entry; however communication with anyone outside who was uninitiated was strictly forbidden. An example of how serious this secrecy was occurred when two teenage boys were caught spying on the rites of the Eleusinian cult. The punishment for those boys was death.

CHAPTER 3

The Birth of Democracy

Moving from mythology back to historical fact, we come to the Athenian Revolution in 508 BC. The people, who had been oppressed for hundreds of years by those in power, revolted against their rulers. The people would find the solution to their trials in one of the most unlikely people.

There are two common approaches to the Athenian Revolution, and both will be taken here in the interest of covering the topic as thoroughly as possible, as this conflict and its resulting governmental changes would change the way that Greece, and subsequently the world, would approach politics. One is to focus on Cleisthenes himself, the other is to look more at the character of the people who fought for their freedom.

Cleisthenes, born around 570 BC, was an aristocrat who, like others of his ilk, had been brought up to be a ruler. He was a descendant of Cleisthenes of Sicyon, a tyrant. The term tyrant in those days didn't neces-

sarily denote corruption; rather it described an absolute ruler. Cleisthenes was born and brought up in a
palatial home, and was reared with the belief that
certain privileges were his by right of his noble birth.

The political climate of Greece during this time period was largely a struggle between city-states to gain
land or influence from another. Oftentimes a polis
(city-state) would be struggling for its independence
from another. Although many aspects of the Greek
city-states were shared, such as the overall religion,
there was no common system of governance, and
each polis was under its own ruler(s).

Athens in the early days of Cleisthenes, as well as
during the Athenian revolution was a relatively small
polis which was led by an individual tyrant. The
tyrant whose corruption led the Athenians to their
historical revolt was Hippias, son of Peisistratus
(Cleisthenes's brother-in-law.)

Peisistratus came to power in Athens by having an
especially tall girl from a neighboring village accom-
pany him to Athens. He claimed that she was Athena
herself, and demanded that he be given rule of the
polis. The people welcomed him as their ruler. Peisistratus, in order to ensure his continued power over
the polis of Athens, appealed to the common people.
He offered the people prosperity by lowering taxes
and doling out free loans, not only to ensure that the

people were in his favor, but also to build up the polis itself.

Under the rule of Peisistratus, Athens was transformed from a smaller rural polis into a center of trade and innovation. The rule of Peisistratus was a great departure from the aristocracy which had dominated Athens and, indeed, most of Greece during this time. Upon his death, tyranny (the rule) of Athens was passed to Peisistratus's son, Hippias.

Hippias began his career much in step with that of his father's rule. He ruled with a modicum of respect and good-treatment of the people of Athens. However, when his brother was murdered, Hippias became paranoid and vitriolic against the people of Athens. He began to execute and banish people who either were, or who he thought were connected with his brother's murder. He took the new freedoms that the people had gained under Peisistratus and replaced it with oppression.

Cleisthenes began his involvement in the revolution of Athens around 510 BC with the intention of seizing power for himself. He had been brought up to further his self-interest, and followed this dictum to its end. Cleisthenes conspired, and succeeded in overthrowing Hippias, and the latter was banished from Athens.

The rule of Cleisthenes was, however, beset by its own conspirators and rivals. The chief rival of Cleisthenes was another Athenian aristocrat named Isagoras. Isagoras had long been involved with the Spartans, and was even rumored to have shared his wife with the king of Sparta. Isagoras appealed to the Spartans to aid him in deposing Cleisthenes, and the Spartans complied.

Sparta, which is most well known for its military prowess, was poised to make Athens a subject of its growing realm of influence. The warlike polis had already dominated its surrounding area for hundreds of square miles, and with Isagoras, a friend of Sparta, as the new ruler of Athens, its influence was set to grow even more.

Fearing the opposition of Cleisthenes and other aristocrats, Isagoras banished Cleisthenes from Athens along with some 700 other households, and it looked like he may never return to his home again. However, having had a taste of freedom under the rule of Peisistratus, the people of Athens revolted against Isagoras and his Spartan allies.

Isagoras and his forces sought refuge in The Acropolis for a period of two days. On the third day, however, he surrendered to the onslaught of the common Athenian people. The citizens of Athens had taken power from the despot (absolute ruler) and had claimed it for themselves. The year was 508 BC. The people recalled Cleisthenes, and the others who had been banished by Isagoras.

It was clear that Cleisthenes could not rule in the manner which had been so common in Athens and various other Greek city-states of the time. It had become apparent that the people must be able to have a say in how they were governed. Cleisthenes ordered a stone meeting area to be carved out of the rock some distance from The Acropolis where the people of the city, commoners and aristocrats alike, could meet and discuss the issues of Athens. It was here that Cleisthenes instituted a simple form of voting. The first instances of the voting process consisted of presenting a white pebble to indicate assent, and a black pebble to indicate disagreement with whatever proposal was before the people.

Issues were brought for a vote every nine days, and these issues encompassed every facet of governance in the polis. This was a pure democracy where the government was one of the people without a separate body to counter or inhibit the decision of the people. Issues such as the declaration of war, raising or lowering taxes, all the way down to the prices of produce and other goods were decided by these democratic votes.

Not only would the advent of democracy give the common people as much of a say in the nature and direction of their government, it would create a system which would change the way that people of the area, and indeed the world after it, would view people's rights, and responsibilities in their own governance. Forms of democracy are still present today, and in its purest forms, it gives people the ability to have an actual, not only a perceived say, in what the government does.

While larger governments that take on a semblance of democracy today often rely heavily on the ideas of a republic (a system where officials are either elected or appointed to represent their individual areas such as representatives in the United States, or members of The House of Commons in Britain,) for the day to day issues and votes, as it would be wildly inefficient to hold votes with the general population every time an issue was presented, the earliest Greek democracy was a direct democracy which did incorporate this widespread influence of the people in every facet of governmental affairs.

The rise of democracy in Athens paved the way for the golden age of Greece. Culture after the advent of democracy in Athens and, subsequently, the rest of Greece flourished in a way that it never had before this time period.

There is evidence of other proto-democratic governments prior to the advent of Athenian democracy, however, the system instituted by Cleisthenes and his fellows was certainly the first of its kind. Not everyone in Athens had the right to vote however. Voting was intended only for adult males, although it's suspected that a voter's family may have had a good deal of influence on his vote.

Another influence that reached voters in a dramatic way (no pun intended) was the satire of the comedic poets of the time. These poets, like artists today, found the ability to sway public opinion in a very real way, and they would often use this power to turn votes to favor their own opinions.

Democracy, although popular among a good share of the people, was considered to be fallacious by many including the great philosopher Plato. Plato believed that unless elected officials were philosophers of the finest thread, Greece would never be free of the evils of ambition and tyranny. Plato favored a kingdom ruled by men of philosophy to ensure continual progress and rescue from the necessary evils contained in men who failed to question.

Another interesting facet of Athenian democracy was that of ostracism. Ostracism, put simply, was the voted ejection of a person from the borders of the city-state. Although the practice had the potential to rid the area of individuals who would be counterproductive to the spread of Greek freedoms, it was often used as a political tool to oust individuals who were unliked by an individual or a group. This process was often unofficially sanctioned for such means, as in the case of Themistocles, the great general who had led the Athenians to many important victories against Persia.

Although Athenian democracy wasn't perfect, it undoubtedly led to the Golden Age of Greece. People were brought together more through this simple invention, the casting of a stone, than they had been in the previous history of the land. Not only culture, but trade, production, the economy, and many other facets of Greek life were enhanced by this revolutionary concept.

CHAPTER 4

Darius, Xerxes, and the Persian Threat

In 492 BC, though the Democracy of Athens was still very young, Athens began to gain a significant amount of power. Athens at the time was still a smaller polis, but it caught the attention of Darius, known as The Great King of The Persian Empire.

The Persian Empire was undoubtedly the greatest power of the day. It was located across the sea to the East of Athens, and stretched from Turkey all the way to India. The Empire was ruled by Darius, a tyrannical leader who demanded unyielding submission. Darius was so feared by his people, and had such a level of dominion over them that those who would beg his favor were required to cover their mouths when in his presence so the air that he breathed would not be contaminated by their presence.

As all dictatorial rulers do, Darius feared the growth in power of any civilization other than his own. When it became clear that Athens was becoming too powerful for Darius's liking, he sent a force to invade.

The first campaign of the Persians against the Greeks was carried out by Mardonius, the son-in-law of Darius. During this campaign, Mardonius's forces conquered and re-subjugated the city of Thrace. Macedon, an ally of the Persians, was also subjugated. This campaign, although having its victories would end after the Persian fleet was lost in a storm near the coast of Mount Athos. After being injured during a raid of his camp, Mardonius returned home.

Darius sent ambassadors to all of the poleis of Greece demanding submission to his rule in 491, and almost all of these city-states complied. In Sparta and Athens, however, not only were the ambassadors refused their submission, but were also killed.

Undoubtedly the most famous event of the war between Darius's Persia and the city-states of Greece was the battle of Marathon. The Persians landed in the polis of Marathon, a city which had no standing army. News of the Persian invasion travelled quickly. The Persian Empire was one of tyranny and slavery, while the Greek city-states were a culture which valued its freedom.

That being so, a herald (or day runner/courier) named Pheidippides was sent from Athens to request the aid of Sparta, the military superpower of the Greek poleis, in dispelling the Persian force from their shores. Pheidippides ran over 150 miles (246 kilometers) in the space of less than two days. This remark-able journey through the countryside of Greece is the origin of modern marathons.

Although Pheidippides performed an astonishing feat by making this desperate run, the Spartans refused the plea for help. Athens would have to defend itself against the Persians.

While Pheidippides was making his run, the Athenians were gathering their forces. Everyone who was able from peasants armed with spears, sticks, or whatever they could find to the hoplites who were citizen-soldiers, able to afford the finer armor. The hoplites were predominantly armed with spears, clad in armor of bronze, and generally had some military training.

Despite being outnumbered two-to-one by the Persian forces, the Greek soldiers won an unlikely victory against their invaders. They killed an estimated 6,000 Persian troops in one day, and scattered their forces.

The victory of the Greeks over the Persians was an incredible blow to Darius. After the loss to the Greeks in the failed first invasion, Darius began amassing yet another enormous army. This army was intended to invade Greece yet again, but it fell into discord when the Egyptians revolted. Darius died while trying to quell this uprising. With Darius's death in 486 BC, control of The Persian Empire was passed to his son Xerxes.

Xerxes was hateful toward the Greeks and the Egyptians, blaming them for the death of his father. The revolt in Egypt was quickly put down by Xerxes, and a new plan to invade Greece was initiated. He decided to bridge Hellespont (modern day Dardanelles) a thin sea strait about .75 miles (1.2 kilometers) at its thinnest point in order for his massive army to cross into Greece.

Many of the Greek poleis pledged to voluntarily join with Xerxes and the Persian Empire when the Persians arrived. This campaign was delayed however, with a new revolt breaking out in Egypt.

Xerxes began to assemble his army after about four years of preparation. Although the Greek historian Herodotus's estimation of the size of the Persian force was most likely exaggerated, (a figure of 200,000 is much more likely than the stated number of 2.5 million) the size of the Persian army was the largest force of its day.

Xerxes sent ambassadors to the Greek city-states demanding food, water, and land as evidence of their submission to his rule. These ambassadors, due to the previous experience with Sparta and Athens, decided to stay away from those two city-states, hoping to prevent them from being prepared for the coming invasion. This plan did not work, however, as other Greek poleis which were opposed to Xerxes rule over their city-states banded together to form an alliance against the Persian onslaught.

Although only about 10% of the roughly 700 different Greek city-states joined, this alliance would become a powerful foreshadowing of Greek unification. At this time, the Greek poleis were loosely affiliated with one another, if at all. Many of these city-states were even at war with one another. Not much is known about the inner-workings of this confederation, however it is known that among the alliance's powers was that of sending troops to a location after consulting the matter.

In 480 BC, a mere six years after his rise to power, Xerxes's army crossed over their pontoon bridges at Hellespont into Greece. The Greek alliance planned to send its troops to defend against Xerxes's advance at the Vale of Tempe, however this plan was abandoned with news of the tactical risks.

Themistocles, a great Athenian general, proposed a second plan. In order to reach the Southern part of Greece, Xerxes would have to funnel his forces through the narrow pass of Thermopylae (hot gateways.) Themistocles suggested that the larger Persian force could be stopped were the Greeks to send its hoplites to block the pass. In addition, the Greek ships would block the sea strait of Artemisium to ensure that the Persian forces couldn't sidestep the pass of Thermopylae by sea.

The plan had a hitch though, as the estimated arrival of the Persian forces to Thermopylae would coincide with not only the Olympic games, but also with the festival of Carneia. Carneia took place between August (the Greek month of Carneus) 7th and the 15th. This was a festival to honor Apollo Carneus, and was of particular importance to the Spartans. Due to the observance of this festival, and the perceived sacrilege implied by committing warfare during this period, the Spartan force consisted only of King Leonidas and his personal bodyguard of 300 men.

The usual hippeus (Spartan royal honor guard) consisted of young men, but as the destruction of his force was all but assured, the guard was replaced by men who had already fathered children. Along with the Spartan force of 301 men (Counting Leonidas,) there was a supporting army of the allies who joined the defense of Thermopylae. Additional forces were gathered along their way.

Upon their arrival at Thermopylae, the allied army rebuilt the Phocian wall at the tightest place in the pass. Xerxes waited for three days for the men to leave the pass. It wasn't until he was finally convinced that this small force intended to hold the hot gateways that Xerxes sent his men to attack.

Despite overwhelming numbers, the allies had a few key elements on their side. Due to the narrowness of the pass, the larger force of the Persian army was forced to meet the phalanx (a close, usually rectangular formation of soldiers) of the Greeks straight on, causing their men to fall quickly at the hands of the superior tactic of the allied army. Also, the Spartans, despite their smaller numbers, were exceptionally well-trained, as they were brought up from childhood to be soldiers. They also had, surprisingly enough, a great amount of morale due to the knowledge that they were choosing to fight (and die) by their own choice, and the invading force was one of slaves and conscripted men.

The allied forces held out against the massive Persian armies for a period of two days until a local man named Ephialtes betrayed them by disclosing a path behind the Greek forces to Xerxes. Leonidas caught wind of the betrayal, and released the larger part of the combined army, keeping only his men and a handful of other volunteers, leaving a grand total of about 2,000 men to cover the retreat of the rest of the forces. According to Herodotus, these men stood defiant against the prospect of certain destruction. Xerxes, not wanting to lose any more of his men, called upon his archers to deliver the final blow against the allied forces at Thermopylae.

Although this battle was lost, one crucial thing came of it. The Greeks began to see that unification could and would be to the benefit of the poleis, so long as these cities were allowed to keep their freedom.

While the battle of Thermopylae was taking place, another impressive battle was being carried out on the seas. Xerxes's navy was engaged in a naval battle against 271 allied Greek triremes. The Greeks were covering the flank of the army at Thermopylae. The allied navy held up against the Persian onslaught for the space of about three days until, hearing of the outcome of the battle at Thermopylae, the damaged allied vessels retreated as they were no longer needed.

After Thermopylae, Xerxes went on to conquer all of Boeotia, and subsequently most of Greece. Themistocles hatched a desperate plan. Before the first battle, he had consulted with the oracle at Delphi. The message from the Delphic oracle was as follows:

"Now your statues are standing and pouring sweat. They shiver with dread. The black blood drips from the highest rooftops. They have seen the necessity of evil. Get out, get out of my sanctum and drown your spirits in woe." (Fontenrose, 1981)

The message was a great blow to the Greeks, however, when consulted again, the oracle gave them a way out:

"A wall of wood alone shall be uncaptured, a boon to you and your children." (Fontenrose, 1981)

The city-state of Athens had no wooden walls at this time, but Themistocles took the second divination as the Greeks' way to victory. He believed that the wall of wood described a force of Greek Triremes, the most advanced ships in the armada. He commissioned hundreds of these ships to be made, and the beginning stages of his plan began to come together.

When Xerxes and his forces advanced toward Athens, Themistocles convinced them to do something drastic. The Athenians evacuated their homes and ultimately their city. Athens fell to the Persians, and their homes, temples, and most of the city was destroyed. Xerxes, frustrated at having received more resistance than he had hoped for, decided that his best bet in ending the conflict quickly was to destroy the Greek armada.

Led by Themistocles, the force of Greek triremes was stationed off the coast of Salamis, and Themistocles put his plan into action. He sent Xerxes a note disguised as a treasonous missive which told Xerxes of the armada's location. What he didn't convey was that the Greeks had hoped for Xerxes's armada to join battle with the Greek triremes in this place because, much like at Thermopylae, the superior Persian numbers would be forced to attack the Greeks in a narrow strait, thereby levelling the playing field.

The plan worked. According to Herodotus, Xerxes sat upon his throne on a beach, watching the naval battle commence. His fleet was torn apart by that of the Greeks, and the battle was lost. It's said that about 200 Persian ships were sunk or captured by the Greek navy, and the battle was a red-letter victory for the forces of Greece.

Xerxes, infuriated at the loss of his naval superiority fled back to his empire, leaving Mardonius, his brother-in-law to complete the subjugation and conquest of Greece. Although the war was not yet over, the Greeks would prevail against the Persian forces, and return to their homes after the battle of Salamis-in-Cyprus.

In 478 BC, The Delian League was formed to ally various poleis against the threat of Persia after the second invasion. Somewhere between 150 and 172 individual city-states came together to form the Delian league. This group got its modern name from their meeting place on the island of Delos. Athens grew rich and powerful through its influence in the league and, much to the chagrin of smaller, less powerful states, grew to a great deal of overall superiority. It wasn't long after the inception of the Delian League Athens took control of the league's navy, and the Athenian proclivity toward heavy-handed tactics for its own interest led to the Peloponnesian War. The league was disbanded at the conclusion of this war.

These years of conflict with the Persians had certainly taken their toll on Greece and its people, however, with victory came a new kind of unification among the Greek poleis, and gave rise to the golden age of Greece.

CHAPTER 5

Pericles and the Golden Age

Also called the classical age, the golden age of Greece lasted between about 480-300 BC. Although the Athenians and the Spartans came together to fight the Persians, they would remain rivals throughout most of their existence in the ancient times.

Much of the history that we have of Greece was recorded by a man named Herodotus (484-409 BC.) He was a historian, in fact, he's often known as the father of history (although Voltaire would later refer to him as the father of lies.) Herodotus was the first known historian to not only retell, or collect history, but to take certain measures to test the authenticity of the stories of the day and of the past.

The golden age of Greece was a veritable explosion of philosophy, art, and architecture. This period was home not only to Herodotus, but to philosophers such as Socrates, Plato, and Aristotle, men whose insights would not only change the thoughts of the day, but live on to affect us in modern times. We will get to them in the next chapter.

Discussion of the golden age of Greece cannot be in any way thorough without taking a look at Pericles. Pericles (495-429 BC) began taking part in politics in Athens around 472 BC. As son to a well-known politician, a man by the name of Xanthippus, Pericles was encouraged at a young age to become involved with politics and government.

Athens was still reeling from the impact of the wars with Persia, and it was a long and difficult process toward rebuilding and restoring order. Pericles saw the wealth that was accruing to Athens through the Delian League, and contrasted this with the fact that Athens had not been fully rebuilt. Rather than add to the force of the navy by manpower, or construction of triremes, many of the city-states in the Delian League elected instead to donate money and other provisions. With this wealth, the city of Athens was poised, not only for rebuilding, but for a large-scale glorification of their city.

Although, after continued campaigns by the Delian League against Persia had rendered the former foe inconsequential as a threat to the Greeks at the time, Pericles insisted that the other members of the dissolving council continue to donate as they had when military campaigns were at their height. Pericles eventually raided the stockpile of wealth at Delos and brought it to his home polis of Athens.

With this influx of wealth, Pericles had the city and its temples restored. Along with this, he commissioned the building of the Parthenon, a site which, although in ruins today, still holds a great deal of interest to Athens and indeed the world. The Parthenon housed an enormous statue of Athena, and was certainly an incomparable testament to the artistry and craftsmanship of the day. No expense was spared, and it is interesting to note that the Parthenon doesn't actually contain any right angles. It was built in such a way as to compensate for the illusion which is created by intersecting lines that makes them appear to bow.

It is often said, as Thucydides once remarked, that Athens during this time was only a democracy in its appearance, while in actuality, it was ruled by Pericles, sometimes known as The First Citizen of Athens.

With the outbreak of the Peloponnesian War, a conflict between Athens and its allies against Sparta and its allies which lasted approximately 30 years, not only would the supremacy of Athens come under fire, but the control of Athens by the Athenians was also culled.

The Peloponnesian war began when Athens made it apparent that Persia was not to fear, Athens was. The parties of the Delian League were taken advantage of by the Athenians and Sparta wasn't willing to trade one dictator abroad for one closer to home. The most complete account of the Peloponnesian war was made by General Thucydides, an aforementioned ally of Pericles.

Athens basically controlled the Delian League however Sparta, never to be outdone, had its own league called The Peloponnesian League. The Peloponnesian League was vast and powerful. When the helots, Sparta's slave class, revolted in 465 BC, Athens sent a force to support the Spartans, however their assistance was refused as Sparta believed the force was intended, not to aid Sparta, but to take advantage of the conflict.

In 449, two members of the Peloponnesian League came into conflict. Athens and Megara formed an alliance and decided to enter into the conflict. This resulted in Spartan forces pitting themselves against Athens, and is often referred to as the First Peloponnesian War. The outcome of this conflict ended in 445 BC with an agreement of peace between the two empires known as the 30 Years Peace. The terms set down basically came down to the Athenian Empire and the Spartan Empires agreeing to not get involved with matters of their respective groups.

The Athenians, however, did not long hold to this agreement and set about involving themselves in acts such as taking over settlements, imposing sanctions, and striking out against the Peloponnesian League at large. Under Pericles, a wall was built between Athens and its port of Piraeus so that Athens, even if besieged by Sparta, would be able to import whatever goods it required from its growing empire, and it would never have to meet the fierce Spartan army on its own terms. Due to Athenian naval superiority, it was able to move much more quickly than the Spartan army, and even bypass it entirely. For this purpose, much of the Spartan force was required to stay in and around Sparta for fear of an Athenian attack. Athens, Pericles theorized, would remain safe so long as it didn't attempt to expand its empire.

Unfortunately for Athens, the construction of this wall encased the citizens of the polis in close quarters, and in a relatively short amount of time, these close quarters along with a lack of general sanitation led to an outbreak of plague which killed an estimated 30,000 Athenian citizens. Pericles himself succumbed to this plague, and died within six months of contracting it.

With the death of Pericles, rule of the city went to various demagogues until Alcibiades took control of the polis. He went against the non-expansion which Pericles had insisted upon and sought to grow the Athenian Empire. Alcibiades led a campaign to take Sicily which was, at that time, under attack from Syracuse. Upon his return, however, Alcibiades went, not back to the Athenians, but to Sparta. His allegiance would switch many times between alliance to Athens and allegiance to Sparta, no doubt weakening the cause of Athens.

Alcibiades was eventually killed, not just for his ambivalent alliances to Greek States, but also at times with Persia. The Athenians were caught in a state of discord as many leaders would follow Alcibiades in their lust for control over the Athenian Empire. Multiple further campaigns were sent to Sicily, and all of them failed, eventually decimating the naval supremacy of Athens. This wouldn't be the last word on the Athenian navy, however, as they built new ships and formed new armies.

Things finally turned after the battle of Arginusae. Although the Athenian fleet had won a great battle, the brilliant naval commanders were executed due to their retreat from a storm in order to save their ships. Without the skilled leadership of these commanders, the Athenian Navy was eventually decimated by a Spartan fleet that sailed in Persian ships. The polis of Athens would eventually be starved into submission.

This Spartan victory led to the end of the war in 404 BC and the eventual subjugation of Athens by Sparta. A group known as the 30 tyrants who led Athens now, not in a democracy as it had been, but an oligarchy (rule by a small group of people.) This oligarchy would not stand however, as Athens was eventually able to retake their city and their democracy about a year after the institution of the 30 tyrants.

This war was costly to both sides, and eventually led to the fall of both poleis to outside forces.

In the north, a city called Macedon was not far from coming to a level of power as yet unknown in Greece, or indeed the world. Macedon had long battled against barbarian invaders, and had fallen into bad a rapport with the more influential city-states of the time. The Macedonians were often considered to be hardly civilized themselves, but it would be the successive reign of one man and his son that would change the political and cultural landscape of the world.

Philip II (382-336 BC) came to power in 359 BC. Philip had a vision for Macedon and for Greece itself. He wasted no time in getting his plans off the ground. The common practice of warfare in Greece at the time was based on the phalanx formation, and Philip's armies were no different in that fundamental aspect. However, it was the development of weaponry, diplomatic relations, and a change to a professional, well trained army that would make these plans possible.

Macedon had lost key battles before Philip II's accession to the throne. Philip was quick to forge alliances with neighboring cities and set about rebuilding the army. He not only rebuilt the army in numbers, but oversaw the development of a few different types of weapons that would make the Macedonian military the envy of the world. One of these weapons was called the sarissa.

The sarissa was a pike, or long spear, up to about 20 feet in length. Used in a phalanx and in conjunction with cavalry units, the sarissa could keep enemy forces at bay and at a distance while they were being flanked. Enemies had nothing to match the length of the sarissa, and were more often than not at the mercy of the Macedonian forces at the tips of these pikes.

Another important innovation was that of the gastraphetes (belly-shooters.) Unlike the traditional bow and arrow that only had as much force as the archer had strength in his arms, gastraphetes were crossbows which harnessed the power of a man's whole body. These weapons were a far sight more powerful and more effective against enemy units, especially in siege operations, than bows and arrows.

Along with sarissas and gastraphetes, two types of torsion ballistae were developed: oxybeles (bolt-shooters) and lithobolos (stone-shooters.) The oxybeles could fling a large bolt to lengths of up to a quarter mile, and easily penetrate enemy armor. The lithobolos could hurl stones up to 180 pounds in weight a great distance, effectively making the Macedonian forces unmatched in distance warfare.

One of Philip's sons, a young man who would grow to join his father on his military campaigns, and eventually become king was named Alexander. Alexander (more commonly referred to as Alexander the Great) came under the tutelage of Aristotle, a well-known and important philosopher at the age of 13.

When his father was battling against Byzantium, Alexander was left in charge. A group called the Maedi staged a revolt against Macedonia, and Alexander was put to an early test. He quickly drove the Maedi from their land and settled his own countrymen in their place and founded Alexandropolis, the first, but far from the last city that Alexander would name for himself.

By 346 BC, Philip's power had grown to a level which, in practice, set him as the leader of Greece. The Greek city-states resented the reach of Philip's power, and began to build their resistance to him. In 338 BC, allied Greek poleis, including Athens and Thebes, fought against Philip and Alexander in the battle of Chaeronea.

Alexander was only 18 at the time of the battle, and when he and his father prevailed against the forces of Athens and Thebes, Philip was in a position to destroy or rule these city-states in whatever way he so desired. In a gesture that was completely unexpected by these conquered city-states, Philip allowed the men to return to their homes and carry on within their cities as they had done before the conflict. Philip loved the culture of Greece, and wished for the territories he had conquered to retain their individuality.

Philip would die in 336 BC, just before mounting his ultimate plan of invading the vast and powerful empire of Persia, at the hands of one of his own bodyguards. During his 20 years ruling Macedon, Philip had made his once looked-down-upon city the seat of the Greek Empire. Alexander, now 20, would take the throne of Macedon.

Being only half-Macedonian himself and having a slew of relatives (Philip had seven wives, only one of which was Macedonian,) Alexander had rivals for the succession to his father's throne. His first order of duty was to remove the contentious parties, many of them by death.

Once secured as king, Alexander followed in his father's footsteps and set out to conquer Greek's longtime enemy of Persia. Before he set off to the east, he put down a number of rebellions, including that of Thebes and Athens.

With the seat of his power secure, Alexander set off for Persia. The Persian Empire stretched from the Middle East to parts of Asia and included portions of

Northern Africa, most notably Egypt. Alexander's task was an enormous one, but he showed his intentions famously by striking a spear into the ground in Asia and proclaimed that he accepted the land as a gift from the gods.

Alexander would win multitudinous victories, cutting his way through the Persian Empire, assaulting Persian cities and harbors, rendering Persian naval forces ineffectual. One of the most impressive victories on his way through the Persian Empire was at the battle of Tyre.

Tyre was a largely fortified city in the Mediterranean Sea that was proving to be difficult to take due to its distance from the shore. The port of Tyre was the last remaining harbor in the region still in his enemy's hands, and so Alexander wasn't about to abandon his campaign against the city.

He made a couple of offers to the Tyrians to avoid full-on conflict. One was that he would leave the people their lives if he was allowed to make a sacrifice at the temple of Melqart, as he equated Melqart with Heracles. He then sent representatives to discuss an agreement of peace, but they were killed and thrown from the city walls into the sea.

Alexander ordered that a siege be staged against the city, and he built a causeway, roughly 2/3 of a mile long (1 kilometer) to the Tyrian shore. With the use of siege towers, he eventually took the city and, frustrated by the stubbornness of the Tyrians, he set fire to the city.

Alexander continued his campaigns and before he was done, he was hailed as King of Macedonia (336-323 BC), Pharaoh of Egypt (332-323 BC), King of Asia (331-323 BC), and King of Persia (330-323 BC.)

Alexander died of an unknown illness in 323 BC. Accounts differ on some of the specifics, such as whether or not he had a fever. There were claims that he was poisoned, but these were largely discounted as he lived for nearly two weeks after taking ill. His military campaigns and his reign over much of the known world would become the stuff of legend.

The Classical Age of Greece effectively came to an end with Alexander's death.

Although this time period was often rife with conflict, it also produced many of the most fantastical wonders of the Greek world. Culture flourished, and many of the Athenian arts, architecture, and philosophies are still something to marvel at to this day.

CHAPTER 6

Philosophy and Discord

Socrates was often described as a plainly ugly man who travelled around wearing a single robe. He was born an Athenian in 469 BC, and would live until his sentence of death by hemlock was carried out in 399 BC. Despite his genius, Socrates was illiterate and therefore his words were collected by Plato and Xenophon, two of his students. Along with his incredible mind, Socrates was also known for his strength, and he fought in the Peloponnesian War.

Although Socrates was an incredibly astute man, when he was proclaimed by the Oracle of Delphi to be the wisest man in all of Athens, he was taken aback, and postulated that either all men must be equally ignorant, or that he was wise by his awareness of his ignorance. His penchant for getting lost in thought was the stuff of legend, and he is claimed to have gotten so wrapped up in his thoughts one day that he stood in one spot, unmoving for the entire length of that day.

His philosophy was one of free-thinking, and questioning the ideas presented through logical processes, each for himself or herself. The Socratic method was a practice of discussion and critical thinking that was intended to question even one's own thoughts and opinions and checking them for their plausibility. Elenchus (proving an idea false by showing its opposite to be true) was the predominant form of Socratic criticism.

In 399 BC, the tyrants of Athens were overthrown. Although Socrates had often shown himself to be a friend to the people of Athens, only suggesting that they look within and without themselves to challenge their beliefs, he was accused of poisoning the minds of the children. He was held for trial, and acted in his own defense. The "courts" of the time were much different than those with which we are familiar today. He was given a brief period in which to defend himself, and used this time to logically prove that he wasn't subject to trial and, in fact, should be honored with free food for the remainder of his life, and held as a benefactor of the people. The judges weren't pleased with his defense and found him guilty, sentencing him to death by hemlock. It was said by his student Xenophon that Socrates's defiance was intentional with the purpose to offend the judges and secure a guilty verdict. According to Xenophon, Socrates believed that he was better off dead.

Socrates was jailed for about a month, but was allowed visitors. The hemlock poison which Socrates was to drink caused an extremely painful death, however when his friends came to him before he drank the poison, he spent his time peacefully discussing the immortality of the soul. Socrates actually had a chance to escape the city, and thus, his sentence, as his friends successfully bribed a guard, but Socrates refused to leave. He reasoned that, even were his verdict to be unfair, it was more important to obey these laws even if it meant his death. Otherwise, the state would have come to harm by this flight from captivity. He willingly drank the hemlock potion dry.

It is postulated by some that Socrates was not in fact a real man, but a creation of Plato. The argument is that Plato formulated the great philosopher in order to give added weight to his own theories. Although there is still debate today about the actual existence of the man named Socrates, the fact remains that his philosophies, whether formulated by himself as a real man, or by Plato as a means to further his own career, have had an enormous impact not only in the time of his life, but throughout the ages, continuing to this day.

Plato (born somewhere between 428 and 423 BC, and died around 347 BC) was a great philosopher and student of Socrates, is quite possibly the most influential philosopher of all time. Plato's prolific written work was not purveyed in the manner to which we are commonly accustomed, but set down as a series of events which usually contained a debate between philosophers.

Plato's ideal government was one where enlightened philosophers would be elevated to the level of kings, as it was only the philosophers who could justly rule. Believing, as Socrates was purported to have said (paraphrased here), that a life without questioning one's beliefs is not a life worth living; it's no leap to understand why Plato favored this form of government, although it would never take form.

One of his predominant philosophies was that of The Theory of Forms. Although this philosophy is now widely discredited, it was often central to Platonic thought. The gist of this philosophy is that what we can perceive is not, in fact, the solid nature of things, but rather (as he would state in the cave analogy) that they are mere shadows *of* the purified forms which are invisible to us.

Plato also believed that knowledge isn't acquired, rather, it is *remembered*. Plato postulated that originally, we had the full and complete knowledge of every aspect of existence, however, we would lose these things and any knowledge that we might gain throughout our lives was a mere remembrance of previously known things.

Although these are a few examples of Platonic thought, this is by no means intended to be a comprehensive list of Plato's philosophy.

A student of Plato, a philosopher by the name of Aristotle (384-322 BC), was regarded to be one of the well-versed philosophers, not only of the ancient world, but of all time. Although, as with many of the ancient philosophers, a large part of his philosophical theories have been discarded, he was and is a very influential man in the field of philosophy. Although a student of Plato, Aristotle rejected the Theory of Forms.

One of Aristotle's philosophies was that of incidental and essential features. For instance, a rock can be black, brown, red, or green and it is still a rock. This would be an example of an incidental feature. However, a rock's composition would be a necessary feature, as a rock made out of feathers would not, in actuality, be a rock.

Aristotle developed a method called formal logic which is still widely used today. The use of formal logic can be illustrated by use of syllogism. This method postulates that new knowledge can be deduced by the combination of previously verified truths. An example would be: All men are six feet tall. John is a man. If John is a man, then he is six feet tall. In this example is also illustrated a further part of formal logic which is that if one of the two propositions is found to be untrue, then the conclusion cannot be said to be necessarily true itself. In this case, it's not true that all men are six feet tall, therefore it can only be deduced from this information that some men may be six-feet tall, but men (including John) aren't necessarily of this height.

Aristotle also believed that any statement could only be true or false. The problem with this philosophy, however, arises when postulating future-oriented statements. If one person says that they were going to walk to the store and randomly meet a tall woman named Daphne and another person said that he would not meet such a woman, but a short man named Bruce then which one of them was telling the truth? Before the event, this is unknowable. Another problem arises if, when arriving at the store, the first person actually does meet a short man named Bruce, this person can't argue that the other was wrong in their statement, even though the result happened out of mere happenstance.

These are but a few examples of a few of the theories of a few of the philosophers of the day. Philosophy during this time was highly revered, and these men (and many others) made an indelible mark on the world with their ideas.

CHAPTER 7

Enter the Roman Empire

Greek sovereignty was not to last forever. Many invaders entered and conquered various states of Greece; however the Roman conquest of Greece would prove the largest empirical change to the region for many years to come.

The Punic wars lasted from 264 to 146 BC and were predominantly a conflict between Rome in modern day Italy and Carthage in northern Africa. Although, during the Third Punic War, the conflict wasn't contained in the land-mass of Greece, the Romans had become increasingly irritated by the agitation of the Greek states.

The growing Roman power had fought many battles within the land of Greece; however, it was the Roman conquest of the city of Corinth that brought things to a head. The Romans fought against the Corinthians and their allies of the second Achaean League, a confederation of Greek city-states in the north-central area of Peloponnese.

The Romans, well known as fierce expansionists, finally took the City of Corinth in 146 BC, and although this was not the immediate end of the Greek empire, it was the first major blow toward this end. Although the Achaean League revolted against its Roman invaders, the onslaught of the Romans was only beginning.

Not only were cities taken, but the Greek religion was absorbed and equated with that of the Romans. Deities such as Zeus, Aphrodite, and Ares were equated with Jupiter, Venus, and Mars respectively. This cultural shift played a big part in the Romanization of the Greek empire.

The Greek Peninsula at large would come under the control of Rome or its prefecture in 146 BC with the Aegean Islands following suit in 133 BC. Greece had long been influential in Roman life and culture. Under the rule of Rome, Greek culture was actually much the same as it had been. This continuity of Greek culture lasted until the arrival of Christianity, even though Greek independence was ended.

Greece and Rome were long intertwined, not necessarily as allied forces, but as a sharing of cultures. This is by no means to suggest that these cultures didn't clash with each other, although there was often a level of give-and-take on this cultural level.

indelible impossible to remove *adj*

imprint :(n)
a distinguishing mark

CONCLUSION

We have arrived at the conclusion of this book. I want to thank you for joining me on this incredible journey through one of the greatest civilizations that our world has ever seen.

History, even ancient history such as this, is important, not only because it tells us where we came from and what affected the world of the past, but it has shaped all of us, Greek or no in our societies and our cultures.

From the philosophers such as Socrates, Plato, and Aristotle to the military leaders such as Thucydides, Leonidas, and Philip II, the times and places associated with Ancient Greece have left their indelible imprint on our world, and indeed, on all of us who live in it. *a impossible distinguishing mark on our world, and include, on all of who live in it*

With history, we find myth and fact, truth and legend about the people who lived during these far away times. We also find in our own civilizations today marks of those seemingly distant times. By looking at the past, we can better understand our present, and plan for a better future with the lessons long ago

Martin   *beautiful writing*

learned, passed down through countless generations of men and women whose own lives form a lineage, a direct connection with those times.

It has been an absolute pleasure to delve into this elegant, often troubled time in the history of the world and share with you a collection of some of the events that took place to shape an incredible empire.

From its humble beginnings to the unprecedented reign of Alexander the Great, Greece has been a fascination of millions of people throughout the ages. I hope that you have enjoyed this journey as much as I have, and I hope that you'll press on with the other histories in this series to discover even more about the civilizations that have set the stage for our modern life.

When we look back into the past, we see ourselves in the cacophony of the times which have preceded our own. Peace and war, enlightenment and ignorance, and the individual journeys of the heroic and the common alike no doubt will continue to shape our world as we move forward, day by day, in our own quests for greatness.

Thank you,

Martin R. Phillips

Alexander the Great

delve delve v.t
　　　to search resolutely

cacophony n. a hash noise
ignorance n lack of experien
　　lack of experienc
　　n knowledge

quests
quest in a search
　　v.t to go on search

A Preview of
Martin R. Phillips'
Latest Book

ANCIENT EGYPT

Ancient Egypt is one of the most fascinating civilizations that the world has ever seen. From looming pyramids to intricate monoliths; from kings and pharaohs to the waters of the Nile, Egypt's history is one in which we can see the potential of humanity.

Even today, while there are some theories, we are not certain how the ancient Egyptians built many of their monuments, including the pyramids. The civilization of Egypt was home to some of the most profound thought of the time, some of the most incredible inventions and some of the most famous rulers throughout history.

So what is it about Ancient Egypt that has fascinated us for millennia and continues to pique our interest today?

There seems to be a unique spirit to the ancient Egyptians. The Egyptian way of life seems to be almost anachronistic in a lot of ways. They had primitive batteries (we still don't know why,) they were fans of board games, women enjoyed more freedom in ancient Egypt than they did in other civilizations, in many cases for thousands of years to come, they had house pets, used a form of chewing gum made from myrrh and wax and some Egyptian doctors actually specialized in different areas of medicine.

Providing exact dates to events in ancient Egypt can be quite difficult, and in some cases impossible, as the ancient Egyptians did not use a standardized system of chronology as we do today. The ancient Egyptians would instead use the length of their pharaohs' reigns as a way of telling the year. While this may have been useful enough at the time, it's difficult for researchers nowadays to pinpoint at exactly which time the fourth year of Khufu was. In most cases we don't know exactly when these pharaohs reigned, or even how close we are to a complete list of pharaohs. Therefore, dates in this book will focus more on a dynastic timeline with modern calendar years being added in where possible.

The history, culture and symbolism of ancient Egypt is still popular today, over two thousand years later. There are many things to be fascinated about in regard to ancient Egypt. But what made them who they were? What drove them to settle where they settled, live how they lived and create such an enigmatic and captivating civilization? How were the Egyptians able to sustain their civilization for nearly three thousand years?

These and many other questions will be covered in these pages. I invite you to sit back, relax and enjoy learning about what is quite possibly the most important and interesting ancient civilizations the world has ever seen...

PS. If you enjoyed this book, please help me out by kindly leaving a review!

Ancient Greece

Made in the USA
Lexington, KY
17 August 2019